Books a

D0716976

Consulting Editors
Ray Monk and Frederic Raphael

THE

GREAT

PHILOSOPHERS

Christopher Johnson

....

DERRIDA

The Scene of Writing

PHŒNIX

A PHOENIX PAPERBACK

First published in Great Britain in 1997 by
Phoenix, a division of the Orion Publishing Group Ltd
Orion House
5 Upper Saint Martin's Lane
London, WC2H 9EA

A catalogue reference is available
from the British Library

ISBN 0 753 80184 1

Typeset by Deltatype Ltd, Birkenhead, Merseyside

Printed in Great Britain by
Clays Ltd, St Ives plc

DERRIDA

The Scene of Writing

Born in the El-Biar district of Algiers in 1930, Jacques Derrida is probably the best known of French philosophers living today. His work has been translated into numerous languages and has been of influence not only in philosophy but in a whole range of humanities-related disciplines: literary and cultural studies, sociology and anthropology, history and legal studies.

It is commonly acknowledged that Derrida's writing can be difficult, this for a number of reasons. First there is the difficulty of the concepts and arguments themselves, a difficulty compounded by the fact of Derrida's training in a continental tradition of philosophy with which non-French readers are not always readily conversant. Second, Derrida's philosophy is not a *systematic* philosophy, that is to say, he does not present the reader with a finished philosophical system in which each term is defined and located, from first principles to final theory. As we shall see, much of his analysis and reasoning is conducted in dialogue with other thinkers, through a process of close reading, citation and commentary. The problem with this approach is that the reader often needs to have some knowledge of these thinkers before he or she can even begin to follow Derrida's arguments with any degree of consistency. A final difficulty is the actual *style* of Derrida's writing. While this is never wilfully opaque, to those used to so-called 'plain' language it can often seem highly rhetorical. For the English-speaking reader, this has partly to do with the sometimes considerable differences in register between English and French, but it is complicated by Derrida's own penchant for paradoxical formulation, neologism and various forms of wordplay. Not surprisingly, this has created many difficulties for foreign translators of his work.

The corpus of Derrida's published work is extensive, covering a period of over thirty years. The aspect of his philosophy I intend to concentrate on in this short study comes from an earlier phase of his work, though the questions and problems it addresses could be seen as being fundamental to his thought: the theory of writing and the mode of philosophical enquiry called 'deconstruction'. These are the two main strands of one of Derrida's most important early texts, *Of Grammatology* (1967),[1] which will be the principal focus of the following commentary. More specifically, the commentary will be concentrating on Derrida's reading and critique of the anthropologist Claude Lévi-Strauss (1908–) in a central chapter of this book, using it as a working example of deconstruction and of the theory of writing.

The task Derrida sets himself in *Of Grammatology* is an ambitious one: to question and contest a tradition of Western thought in which writing has consistently been cast in a role subordinate to that of speech. Whereas speech is habitually associated with reason and rationality (the Greek notion of *logos*) and the voice is perceived as being closer to the inner 'truth' of individual consciousness, writing is considered to be a secondary extension or supplement to the voice, an auxiliary technology employed by human reason but not essential to it. Speech is the guarantor of presence and of authenticity, whereas writing

4

represents artifice and absence, the alienation and deferment of presence. In *Of Grammatology*, Derrida's critique of
this historical subordination of writing, which he calls
'logocentrism', takes the form of close, sustained readings
of thinkers representing different instances or 'moments' of
the logocentric tradition, the most substantial of which are
the readings devoted to Saussure, Lévi-Strauss and Jean-
Jacques Rousseau.

Derrida's choice of Saussure and especially of Lévi-Strauss
as examples of logocentrism was not an arbitrary one, if
one takes into account the very particular context of France
in the 1960s. Ferdinand de Saussure (1897–1913) is normally regarded as the founder of modern linguistics. He is
credited with having transformed linguistics from a pre-
dominantly historical and comparative discipline into a
rigorous science, with its own specific programme and
methods of analysis. Saussure argued that language is a
system, in which it is the relations between elements and
not the elements themselves that are responsible for
meaning. An individual word, for example, only makes
sense in terms of its *difference*, phonetically and conceptu-
ally, from other words: meaning is differential, while the
terms (phonetic elements, words, etc.) in themselves are
arbitrary. According to Saussure, the task of the linguist was
to investigate the deep-level structures which governed the
differential relations between the constituent elements of
language, rather than the contingent and mutable realiza-
tions of these structures, such as one would find in the
everyday production of language. Lévi-Strauss's innovation
was to argue that the different social practices and institu-
tions studied by anthropologists, for example kinship
structures or mythological representations, could be treated

as a kind of second-order language, amenable to the same kind of analysis Saussure had pioneered in linguistics. The task of the anthropologist would be to discern the deep-level structures to which these different social phenomena would be reducible.

Lévi-Strauss's structural anthropology was extremely influential in France during the 1950s and 1960s, inspiring a whole range of disciplines, from history and philosophy to psychoanalysis and literary studies, and thus initiating the movement that came to be known as 'structuralism'. Equally important was the description of these disciplines as the 'human sciences'. As precisely *sciences* of the human, the human sciences claimed to have left behind the metaphysical preoccupations of traditional philosophy and to be offering both a more concrete and more scientific perspective on the totality of human experience. The traditional role of philosophy as the privileged point of synthesis of human knowledge – both scientific and humanistic – thus seemed increasingly redundant: the human sciences had no need of this kind of philosophy, and could think for themselves. There was therefore a strong sense at this time that philosophy had been displaced from its traditional position at the centre of humanistic enquiry, while structuralism and the new human sciences swept all before them. Jean-Paul Sartre's version of existentialism, which had more or less dominated intellectual debate in France since the war, suddenly appeared limited and outdated. Lévi-Strauss himself attacked the subjectivist bias of existentialism: a philosophy based on personal experience, he argued, can never tell us anything essential about society or humanity, but is simply a dramatization of the individual. Moreover, he criticized the ethnocentrism of a philosophy whose conception of the individual subject was entirely culture-specific and thus far from achieving the universality it claimed.

Given the context just described, Derrida's readings of Saussure and Lévi-Strauss in *Of Grammatology* should therefore be seen as a necessary and important intervention in the debate which developed around structuralism in the 1960s. Surprisingly, perhaps, his commentary and critique of Lévi-Strauss concentrates not on the latter's theoretical work, as described above, but on a text which is primarily an autobiography, *Tristes tropiques*, published in 1955. *Tristes tropiques* was Lévi-Strauss's personal account of his initiation into anthropology, his fieldwork studies undertaken in Brazil in the 1930s, and more generally his experience of a changing world in the interwar and postwar years. This was interspersed with passages of straight ethnographic description, sometimes directly transposed from Lévi-Strauss's academic work, and more general, philosophical reflection on the meaning and possible mission of anthropology in relation to the West's continuing transformation of global culture.

Derrida is particularly interested in *Tristes tropiques* because it is in one of its 'ethnographic' chapters, devoted to a South-American Indian tribe called the Nambikwara, that Lévi-Strauss advances what to all intents and purposes is a *theory* of writing. As Derrida shows, this theory does not stand alone as an isolated, self-enclosed formulation, but is part of a whole demonstration that both prepares and justifies it. The structure and register of this demonstration is narrative rather than argumentative, and takes the form of two exemplary scenes involving the ethnologist and his subjects, both recounted in a chapter named 'A Writing Lesson'. The first scene describes how, as a routine part of his field research, the ethnologist distributes paper and pencils among the small Nambikwara group he is staying with, in order to observe and record their reactions. The Nambikwara, he informs the reader, do not know how to write, nor do they draw, apart from certain point or zigzag patterns decorated onto the shells of their gourds. He is therefore surprised when after a few days they begin drawing horizontal, undulating lines on the paper. He assumes that they are attempting to imitate his own writing and drawing as they would have observed it, but notes that they progress no further than this imitation. The chief of the small group, on the other hand, appears to be more enterprising, and alone among his people seems to have understood the function of writing. When working with the ethnologist, he scribbles meaningless lines on his pad in imitation of his guest, and pretends that these lines possess a sense, which he then proceeds to read out.

This apparently harmless scene is the explanatory prelude to a second, more ambivalent and violently charged scene, recounted in the same chapter. The ethnologist has asked the chief to take him to other, related, Nambikwara groups so that he can draw up a complete demographic record of the tribe. When the chief, his group, and the ethnologist arrive, the extreme hostility of the other groups to the presence of the foreigners is barely concealed. To calm the situation, the chief insists that they proceed immediately with the customary exchange of gifts. It is at this point that he takes out his pad and begins to read – or rather, pretend to read – the list of gifts to be exchanged between the groups. This 'comedy', as Lévi-Strauss describes it, lasts for two hours.

The ethnologist himself is both irritated and troubled by this scene, and it is only later, at night, unable to sleep, that he thinks he is able to explain the reason for his unease. I quote Derrida quoting Lévi-Strauss:

> The symbol had been borrowed, but the reality remained quite foreign to them. Even the borrowing had had a sociological, rather than an intellectual object: for it was not a question of knowing specific things, or understanding them, or keeping them in mind, but merely of enhancing the prestige and authority of one individual – or one function – at the expense of the rest of the party. A native, still in the period of the stone age, had realized that even if he could not himself understand the great instrument of understanding he could at least make it serve other ends. (127; 185)

There follows a long passage in which Lévi-Strauss speculates on the historical function of writing and its role in social and cultural change. In sequence, these are the main points of his argument:

• For thousands of years and even today, writing has been the privilege of a powerful elite.

• The considerable transformations in human existence brought about by the use of writing, with its capacity for the almost infinite extension and amplification of human memory, should not blind us to the fact that one of the most crucially productive periods of human prehistory, upon which all of civilization's subsequent achievements rest – the Neolithic – took place in the absence of any known system of writing.

• The period between the invention of writing and the expansion of modern science in the nineteenth century was a period of relative stagnation in which the quantity of knowledge fluctuated rather than increased.

• The only constant historical correlate of the appearance of writing is the formation of cities and empires with a high degree of caste and class differentiation. The primary function of written communication is therefore to enslave and subordinate. The intellectual or aesthetic dimension of writing, its use in the disinterested pursuit of knowledge, is secondary to this function.

• The spread of literacy in Western countries was accompanied by the extension of state control – for example the introduction of military service – and a process of proletarianization. Internationally, the exportation of Western knowledge to newly independent states can be an instrument of mystification and manipulation.

Lévi-Strauss considers the effects of the globalization of Western literate culture to be essentially irreversible. However, in the case of his Nambikwara subjects, there is provisional respite from the alienation of the written word. The sequel to the chief's attempted manipulation of his people completes the 'demonstration'. Again, I quote Derrida quoting Lévi-Strauss:

> Those who moved away from him, after he had tried to play the civilized man (after my visit he was abandoned by most of his followers), must have had a confused

understanding of the fact that writing, on this its first appearance in their midst, had allied itself with falsehood; and so they had taken refuge, deeper in the bush, to win themselves a respite. (134; 195)

It has been necessary to recount in detail the elements of the 'Writing Lesson', as Derrida calls it, because Derrida's critique of Lévi-Strauss and of his theory of writing is itself a close and careful analysis of the *structure* of Lévi-Strauss's demonstration, quoting at length from his text and pondering its detail. As Derrida remarks, the entire demonstration is artfully constructed, and belongs to a recognizable tradition of literary discourse:

In accordance with eighteenth-century tradition, the anecdote, the page of confessions, the fragment from a journal are knowledgeably put in place, calculated for the purposes of a philosophical demonstration of the relationships between nature and society, ideal society and real society, most often between the *other* society and our *society*. (113; 166)

The scene describing the chief's apparent exploitation of writing is itself like a parable:

The story is very beautiful. It is in fact tempting to read it as a parable in which each element, each semanteme, refers to a recognized function of writing: hierarchization, the economic function of mediation and of capitalization, participation in a quasi-religious secret; all this, verified in any phenomenon of writing, is here assembled, concentrated, organized in the structure of an exemplary event or a very brief sequence of fact and

11

gestures. All the organic complexity of writing is here collected within the simple focus of a parable. (126; 184)

More generally, Derrida argues, the sense of violation that accompanies the narrating of this scene is prepared and enhanced by the ethnologist's previous characterization of the Nambikwara as essentially *good*:

> The Nambikwara, around whom the 'Writing Lesson' will unfold its scene (...) the Nambikwara, who do not know how to write, are *good*, we are told. The Jesuits, the Protestant missionaries, the American anthropologists, the technicians on the Line, who believed they perceived violence or hatred among the Nambikwara are not only mistaken, they have probably projected their own wickedness upon them. And even provoked the evil that they then believed they saw or wished to perceive. (116; 170)

Against the negative portrayals of the other visitors to the tribe mentioned above, Lévi-Strauss offers his own personal testimony of the humanity and innocence of this people in the form of a poetic description, scribbled down as he observes the Nambikwara camp at night. Again, Derrida quotes Lévi-Strauss directly:

> When I myself had known them, the diseases introduced by white men had already decimated them; but there had not been, since Rondon's always humane endeavours, any attempt to enforce their submission. I should prefer to forget Mr Oberg's harrowing description and remember the Nambikwara as they appear in a page from my notebooks. I wrote it one night by the light of

my pocket-lamp: 'The camp-fires shine out in the darkened savannah. Around the hearth which is their only protection from the cold, behind the flimsy screen of foliage and palm-leaves which had been stuck into the ground where it will best break the force of wind and rain, beside the baskets filled with the pitiable objects which comprise all their earthly belongings, the Nambikwara lie on the bare earth. Always they are haunted by the thought of other groups, as fearful and hostile as they are themselves, and when they lie entwined together, couple by couple, each looks to his mate for support and comfort and finds in the other a bulwark, the only one he knows, against the difficulties of every day and the meditative melancholia which from time to time overwhelms the Nambikwara. The visitor who camps among the Indians for the first time cannot but feel anguish and pity at the sight of a people so totally dis-provided for; beaten down into the hostile earth, it would seem, by an implacable cataclysm; naked and shivering beside their guttering fires. He gropes his way among the bushes, avoiding where he can the hand, or the arm, or the torso that lies gleaming in the firelight. But this misery is enlivened by laughing whispers. Their embraces are those of couples possessed by a longing for a lost oneness, their caresses are in no wise disturbed by the footfall of a stranger. In one and all there may be glimpsed a great sweetness of nature, a profound nonchalance, an animal satisfaction as ingenuous as it is charming, and, beneath all this something that can be recognized as one of the most moving and authentic manifestations of human tenderness. (116–17; 170–1)

13

Derrida concedes that one might leave this emotive description in its generic category, as simply a personal confession of affection and human solidarity, as a part of autobiographical rather than anthropological discourse; nevertheless, it is integral to the structure of Lévi-Strauss's demonstration:

> The 'Writing Lesson' follows this description, which one may indeed read for what it claims, at the outset, to be: a page 'from my notebooks' scribbled one night in the light of a pocket lamp. It would be different if this moving painting were to belong to an anthropological discourse. However, it certainly sets up a premise – the goodness or innocence of the Nambikwara – indispensable to the subsequent demonstration of the conjoint intrusion of violence and writing. Here a strict separation of the anthropological confession and the theoretical discussion of the anthropologist must be observed. (117; 171)

Personal confession and theory are therefore complicit. It is only by first constructing an idealized image of the Nambikwara as an innocent and simple people that Lévi-Strauss is then able to offer the 'Writing Lesson' as an example or parable of the corrupting effects of writing. Derrida:

> That is why I have followed the description of the innocence of the Nambikwara at length. Only an innocent community, and a community of reduced dimensions (a Rousseauist theme that will soon become clearer), only a micro-society of non-violence and freedom, all the members of which can by rights remain within range of an immediate and transparent, a

14

'crystalline' address, fully self-present in its living speech, only such a community can suffer, as the surprise of an aggression coming *from without*, the insinuation of writing, the infiltration of its 'ruse' and of its 'perfidy'. Only such a community can import *from abroad* 'the exploitation of man by man'. (119; 174)

Having underlined the rhetorical and narrative dimension of Lévi-Strauss's theory of writing, how the theory is in fact demonstrated and justified before its actual enunciation, Derrida then goes on to criticize its conceptual content. His critique is a sweeping one, questioning in their turn each of its separate components. First, he notes the disproportion between the uncertain and ambiguous episode involving the chief's subterfuge (what Lévi-Strauss describes as an 'extraordinary incident') and the theory it is supposed to illustrate:

It is the split between the factual certainty and its interpretative reconsideration that will be of special interest to us. The most serious split appears first, but not only, between the meagre fact of the 'extraordinary incident' and the general philosophy of writing. The point of the incident in effect supports an enormous theoretical edifice. (126; 184)

He then proceeds to question the 'epigenetism' of Lévi-Strauss's interpretation of the 'Writing Lesson', that is, his presentation of writing as something whose appearance is sudden and spontaneous, an external intrusion rather than a development internal to Nambikwara society:

The appearance of writing is *instantaneous*. It is not prepared for. Such a leap would prove that the possibility of writing does not inhabit speech, but the outside of speech. 'So writing had made its appearance among the Nambikwara! But not at all, as one might have supposed, as the result of a laborious apprenticeship.' From what does Lévi-Strauss arrive at this epigenetism that is indispensable if one wishes to safeguard the exteriority of writing to speech? From the incident? But the scene was not the scene of the origin, but only that of the imitation of writing. Even if it were a question of writing, what has the character of suddenness here is not the passage to writing, the invention of writing, but the importation of an already constituted writing. It is a borrowing and an artificial borrowing. As Lévi-Strauss himself says: 'The symbol had been borrowed, but the reality remained quite foreign to them.' Besides, this character of suddenness obviously belongs to all the phenomena of the diffusion or transmission of writing. It could never describe the appearance of writing, which has, on the contrary, been laborious, progressive, and differentiated in its stages. And the rapidity of the borrowing, when it happens, presupposes the previous presence of the structures that make it possible. (126–7; 184–5)

As Derrida indicates here, Lévi-Strauss's parable of writing is itself based on a fiction, the chief's fictional use or abuse of writing. This is not a real writing, as it would have naturally evolved over time within a given social and cultural space, but a spontaneous imitation of writing, which has not been understood. This truncated and caricatural representation of the use of writing in effect allows Lévi-Strauss to distinguish between its intellectual and sociological function:

Since they learned without understanding, since the Chief used writing effectively without knowing either the way it functioned or the content signified by it, the end of writing is political and not theoretical, '*sociological, rather than ... intellectual*'. This opens and covers the entire space within which Lévi-Strauss is now going to think writing. (127; 185)

The distinction is, however, a problematic one:

Distinguishing thus 'the sociological' from the 'intellectual end', attributing the former and not the latter to writing, one credits a very problematic difference between intersubjective relationship and knowledge (...)

Thus suggesting what he will later confirm, that the essential function of writing is to favour the enslaving power rather than 'disinterested' science, according to the distinction he seems to hold, Lévi-Strauss now can, in a second wave of meditation, neutralize the frontier between peoples without and with writing; not with regard to the use of writing, but with regard to what is supposed to be deducible from it, with regard to their historicity or nonhistoricity (...)

Thus, given this trust in the presumed difference between knowledge and power, it is a matter of showing that writing is not at all pertinent to the appreciation of historical rhythms and types; the age of the wholesale creation of social, economic, technical, political, and other structures, upon which we still subsist – the neolithic age – did not know writing. (127–8; 185–6)

Derrida questions the proposition that writing is not an essential condition of science and progress, in support of which Lévi-Strauss has cited the example of the Neolithic revolution:

> That one take no notice of the idea and the project of science, of the idea, that is, of truth as a theoretically infinite transmissibility; this has an historical possibility only with writing (...) Lévi-Strauss's proposal can be sustained only by denying all specificity to the scientific project and to the value of truth in general. This last position does not lack force, but it cannot show the worth and coherence of that force except by relinquishing its claim to be a scientific discourse. A well-known pattern. It is in *fact* what seems to be happening here (...)
>
> That the Neolithic, to which in fact may be attributed the creation of the deep structures upon which we still live, did not know anything like writing. It is here that the concept of writing, as it is used by a modern anthropologist, would seem singularly narrow. Anthropology today gives us a great deal of information about scripts that preceded the alphabet, about other systems of phonetic writing or systems quite ready to be phoneticized. The weight of this information makes it unnecessary for us to insist. (128–9; 187–8)

Lévi-Strauss's affirmation that the rate of accretion of knowledge remained relatively static between the invention of writing and the birth of modern science is criticized for its *empiricity*, that is, it poses an essentially unverifiable question and fails to ask the properly essential question concerning the nature of learning and knowledge:

One could be shocked by this affirmation, but I shall avoid that. I do not believe that such an affirmation is *false*. But no more do I believe that it is *true*. It is rather an answer, suiting a particular purpose, to a meaningless question. Is not the notion of the quantity of knowledge suspect? What is a quantity of knowledge? How is it modified? Without speaking of the science of order or of quality, we may wonder what the quantity of the science of pure quantity signifies. How can it be evaluated in quantity? Such questions can only be answered in the style of pure empiricity. Unless one attempts to respect the very complex laws of the capitalization of learning, something that cannot be done without considering writing more attentively. One can say the opposite of what Lévi-Strauss says and it would be neither truer nor more false. One can say that during such and such a half-century, even before 'modern science', and today every minute, the accretion of knowledge has gone infinitely beyond what is was for millennia. So much for accretion. As for the notion of fluctuation, it presents itself as perfectly empirical. In any case, propositions of essence can never be made to fit a scale. (129; 188–9)

As for Lévi-Strauss's designation of the nineteenth century as the crucial turning point in modern science, Derrida considers that:

It is the most disconcerting step in the development of this paragraph. Let us suppose that the advent of writing three or four thousand years ago had brought nothing decisive in the domain of knowledge. Lévi-Strauss concedes nevertheless that it has not at all been the same thing for the last two centuries. However, according to his own scale, it is not clear what justifies this cut-off point. Yet it is there: 'Doubtless the scientific expansion of the nineteenth and twentieth centuries could hardly have occurred, had writing not existed. But this condition, however necessary, cannot in itself explain that expansion.' Not only is the cut-off point surprising, but one also wonders what particular objection Lévi-Strauss seems to reject here. No one has ever thought that writing – the written notation, since that is at issue here – was the sufficient condition of science; and that it would suffice to know how to write in order to be learned. Much has been written that would suffice to rid us of this illusion if we possessed it. But to recognize that writing is the 'necessary condition' of science, that there is no science without writing, is what is important, and Lévi-Strauss knows this. And as it is difficult in any rigorous way to place the beginnings of science in the nineteenth century, his entire argument founders on or is contaminated by the gross mark of empirical approximation. (129–30; 189)

As Derrida points out, Lévi-Strauss's attempt to distinguish between the intellectual and sociological functions of writing, to dissociate the possibility of scientific progress from the technology of written communication, is the necessary precondition of his hypothesis concerning the oppressive and exploitative function of writing. He continues:

In truth this depends – and that is why I pass over this argument quickly – on the fact that Lévi-Strauss is determined to abandon this terrain, to explain very quickly why the problem of science is not the best access to the origin and function of writing: 'If we want to correlate the appearance of writing with certain other characteristics of civilization, we must look elsewhere.' Thus it must rather be demonstrated that, according to the dissociation which had perplexed us, the origin of writing responded to a more 'sociological' than 'intellectual' necessity. The following pages must therefore not only make clear this sociological necessity – which would be a poor truism and would have little enough to do with the sociological specificity of writing – but also that this social necessity is that of 'domination', 'exploitation', 'enslavement', and 'perfidy'. (130; 189–90)

Derrida does not entirely refute Lévi-Strauss's argument concerning the association of writing, hierarchization and exploitation, but thinks that such an argument would require considerable qualification:

To read this page appropriately, one must differentiate it into its strata. The author presents here what he calls his 'hypothesis': 'If my hypothesis is correct, the primary function of writing, as a means of communication, is to facilitate the enslavement of other human beings.' On a first level, this hypothesis is so quickly confirmed that it hardly merits its name. These facts are well known. It has long been known that the power of writing in the hands of a small number, caste, or class, is always contemporaneous with hierarchization (...) it is at the same time distinction into groups, classes, and levels of economico-politico-technical power, and delegation of authority, power deferred and abandoned to an organ of capitalization. This phenomenon is produced from the very onset of sedentarization, with the constitution of stocks

21

at the origin of agricultural societies. Here things are so patent that the empirical illustration that Lévi-Strauss sketches could be infinitely enriched. This entire structure appears as soon as a society begins to live as a society, that is to say from the origin of life in general, when, at very heterogeneous levels of organization and complexity, it is possible to *defer presence*, that is to say *expense* or consumption, and to organize production, that is to say *reserve* in general. This is produced well before the appearance of writing in the narrow sense, but it is true, and one cannot ignore it, that the appearance of certain systems of writing three or four thousand years ago was an extraordinary leap in the history of life (...)

Previously the empirical character of the analyses concerning the status of science and the accumulation of knowledge removed all rigour from each of the propositions advanced and permitted their consideration with an equal pertinence as true or false. It is the pertinence of the question which appeared doubtful. The same thing happens here again. What is going to be called *enslavement* can equally legitimately be called *liberation*. And it is at the moment that this oscillation is *stopped* on the signification of enslavement that the discourse is frozen into a determined ideology that we would judge disturbing if such were our first preoccupation here.

In this text, Lévi-Strauss does not distinguish between hierarchization and domination, between political authority and exploitation. The tone that pervades these reflections is of an anarchism that deliberately confounds law and oppression. The idea of law and positive right,

although it is difficult to think them in their formality –
where it is so general that ignorance of the law is no
defence – before the possibility of writing, is determined
by Lévi-Strauss as constraint and enslavement. Political
power can only be the custodian of an unjust power. A
classical and coherent thesis, but here advanced as self-
evident, without opening the least bit of critical dialogue
with the holders of the other thesis, according to which
the generality of the law is on the contrary the condition
of liberty in the city. (130–1; 190–1)

It is not necessary to quote here the remainder of
Derrida's point-by-point critique of Lévi-Strauss: the passages cited above give the reader a sufficient idea of the
approach and tenor of this critique. What we learn from
these passages is that Derrida's *deconstruction* of Lévi-
Strauss's theory of writing – his patient analysis of its
different levels and articulations, of its rhetorical as well as
its conceptual framework – is not intended simply to
neutralize and dismiss that theory. First, although Derrida
convincingly exposes the logical inconsistencies and conceptual limitations of Lévi-Strauss's argument, he is above
all interested in the *desire* which animates that argument,
the desire that a binary, black and white distinction should
exist between speech and writing, the former as the
medium of authentic and proximate communication and
the latter as the unnatural and violent alienation of the
voice. This distinction, implicitly rather than explicitly
articulated in Lévi-Strauss's text, repeats what throughout
Of Grammatology Derrida shows to be a consistent reflex of
logocentric philosophy. In an earlier passage of the book,
for example, he shows how Saussure makes a similar

distinction and a similar exclusion of writing, when defining the object and scope of the new science of linguistics:

> In fact, the condition for the scientificity of lingustics is that the field of linguistics have hard and fast frontiers, that it be a system regulated by an internal necessity, and that in a certain way its structure be closed. The representativist concept of writing facilitates things. If writing is nothing but the 'figuration' of the language, one has the right to exclude it from the interiority of the system (for it must be believed that there is an *inside* of the language), as the image may be excluded without damage from the system of reality. Proposing as his theme 'the representation of language by writing' Saussure thus begins by positing that writing is 'unrelated to [the] (…) inner system' of language. External/internal, image/reality, representation/presence, such is the old grid to which is given the task of outlining the domain of a science. (33; 50)

Not only is writing not essential to the constitution of linguistics as a science, but in Saussure's view there has also been an inversion, a perversion of its normal and natural relationship with verbal communication:

> For Saussure, to give in to the 'prestige of the written form' is, as I have just said, to give in to *passion*. It is passion – and I weigh my word – that Saussure analyses and criticizes here, as a moralist and a psychologist of a very old tradition. As one knows, passion is tyrannical and enslaving: 'Philological criticism is still deficient on one point: it follows the written language slavishly and neglects the living language.' 'The tyranny of writing',

Saussure says elsewhere. That tyranny is at bottom the mastery of the body over the soul, and passion is a passivity and sickness of the soul, the moral perversion is *pathological*. The reciprocal effect of writing on speech is 'wrong', Saussure says, 'such mistakes are really pathological'. (38; 56–7)

According to Derrida, there is a structural homology between the historically distinct instances of Saussure, Lévi-Strauss and Rousseau, who each in their own ways are unable to tolerate what they perceive to be the inauthentic and alienating supplement of writing. In this sense, these authors are symptoms of a 'historical structure' a 'problem' which is more general than the authors themselves.

The second point to make about Derrida's deconstruction of Lévi-Strauss's theory of writing is that it shows how the theory itself raises more questions than it answers, questions on the essence of writing, on what writing actually *is*. In his haste to prove that the appearance of writing inevitably entails the corruption of authentic human intercourse, Lévi-Strauss fails to ask the fundamental question as to the nature of the object he is describing, taking as immediately clear and self-evident that he and his reader know and understand what writing is. As we have seen, Derrida questions Lévi-Strauss's assumption that Neolithic culture did not possess a system of writing, as this assumption is based on a singularly narrow conception of writing – Western, alphabetical (phonetic) writing – which, Derrida points out, is but one of a whole number of possible systems of notation. The same criticism is levelled at Lévi-Strauss's characterization of the Nambikwara (whose level of cultural development he compares with that of the

Neolithic) as a 'people without writing'. To be sure, the Nambikwara do not 'write' in the same manner as the ethnologist writes in his notepad – they visibly do not possess a system of phonetic notation –, but Lévi-Strauss is too precipitate, argues Derrida, in his consequent categorization of this people as 'nonliterate'. He asks, for example, 'up to what point it is legitimate not to call by the name of writing those "few dots" and "zigzags" on [the Nambikwara's] calabashes, so briefly evoked in *Tristes tropiques*' (110; 161–2). He also questions the ethnologist's ascription of a purely aesthetic function to the Nambikwara's drawings:

In this operation, which consists of 'drawing lines' and which is thus incorporated into the dialect of this subgroup, Lévi-Strauss finds an exclusively 'aesthetic' signification: 'They called the act of writing iekariuked-jutu, namely "drawing lines", which had an aesthetic interest for them'. One wonders what the import of such a conclusion could be and what the specificity of the aesthetic category could signify here. Lévi-Strauss seems not only to presume that one can isolate aesthetic value (which is clearly most problematic, and in fact it is the anthropologists more than anyone else who have put us on guard against this abstraction), but also to suppose that in writing 'properly speaking', to which the Nambikwara would not have access, the aesthetic quality is extrinsic. Let us merely mention this problem. Moreover, even if one did not wish to treat the meaning of such a conclusion with suspicion, one could still be troubled by the paths that lead to it. The anthropologist has arrived at this conclusion through a sentence noted in *another* subgroup: 'Kihikagnere mũ‿iene' translated by 'drawing lines, that's pretty'. To conclude from this proposition thus translated and recorded within another group (b1), that drawing lines held for group (a1) an 'aesthetic interest', which implies *only* an aesthetic interest, is what poses problems of logic that once again we are content simply to mention. (124; 181)

As Derrida remarks, the normal, critical reflex of the anthropologist would be to caution against categorizations of this type. A properly relativistic approach to other cultures would hesitate to classify this or that cultural artefact or social activity as either 'aesthetic' or 'utilitarian', since such classification runs the risk of projecting onto those cultures categories and distinctions purely our own. In this sense, Derrida argues, Lévi-Strauss's categorization of the Nambikwara from the point of view of Western, phonetic writing – his *phonocentrism* – is ethnocentric, it does not sufficiently relativize the category of writing.

In fact, Derrida points to another possible level of 'writing', which Lévi-Strauss does not recognize as such, and which is described in his 1948 thesis on the Nambikwara but not in *Tristes tropiques*:

When, in *Tristes tropiques*, Lévi-Strauss remarks that 'the Nambikwara could not write . . . they were also unable to draw, except for a few dots and zigzags on their calabashes', because, helped by instruments furnished by them, they trace only 'wavy horizontal lines' and that 'with most of them, that was as far as they got', these notations are brief. Not only are they not to be found in the thesis, but, in fact, eighty pages further on, the thesis presents the results at which certain Nambikwara very quickly arrived and which Lévi-Strauss treats as 'a cultural innovation inspired by our own designs'. It is not merely a question of representational designs showing a man or a monkey, but of diagrams describing, explaining, writing, a genealogy and a social structure. And that is a decisive phenomenon. It is now known, thanks to unquestionable and abundant information, that the birth of writing (in the colloquial sense) was nearly everywhere and most often linked to genealogical anxiety. The memory and oral tradition of generations, which sometimes goes back very far with peoples supposedly 'without writing', are often cited in this connection (. . .) Here [the] function [of writing] is to conserve and give to a genealogical classification, with all that that might imply, a supplementary objectification of another order. So that a people who accede to the genealogical pattern accede also to writing in the colloquial sense, understand its function and go much farther than *Tristes tropiques* gives it to be understood ('that was as far as they got'). (124–5; 181–2)

Of course, Lévi-Strauss's selective restriction of writing to its Western, alphabetic variant is a function of his desire that there exist on the one hand an innocent and ideal community untouched by the script, and on the other a pervasive and corrosive civilization whose power – whose science – is dependent on it. Paradoxically, Derrida shows, it is part of his critique as an anthropologist of the ethnocentrism of Western civilization and its creation of a global monoculture:

The traditional and fundamental ethnocentrism which, inspired by the model of phonetic writing, separates writing from speech with an axe, is thus handled and thought of as anti-ethnocentrism. It supports an ethico-political accusation: man's exploitation by man is the fact of writing cultures of the Western type. Communities of innocent and unoppressive speech are free from this accusation. (121; 177)

Lévi-Strauss's theory of writing therefore commits what one might call an error of punctuation, that is, his framing of the context of writing is an unduly restrictive one, resulting from a limited conceptualization of what writing *in general* might be. An important result of Derrida's deconstruction of this construction is to extend the frame of reference around the phenomenon we normally call 'writing': the 'decorations' on the calabashes, the drawings the Nambik-wara present to the ethnologist, the genealogical tree sketched on the soil – could not all of these be deemed forms of writing, coding, memorization?

However, Derrida's extension of the field of writing is still more radical and more fundamental than the different arguments resumed above. At the same time as he deconstructs Lévi-Strauss's theory of writing, he also advances what in essence is his own theory of writing. So far, in fact, we have only considered cases of what Derrida calls *empirical* writing, writing as it appears to us here and now, in the world, a visible and tangible object – inscriptions on paper, stone, shell or soil, for example. This is what one might call the *manifest* scene of writing, writing as a technology of coding, communication and archivation, writing as an instrumental supplement to verbal communication and the exercise of so-called 'natural' or 'spontaneous' memory. The 'writing' which Derrida goes on to formulate is at once more general and more abstract than the various forms of empirical inscription he rescues from Lévi-Strauss's ethnocentric (phonocentric) demarcations. Increasingly, his questioning of Lévi-Strauss's theory of writing becomes a questioning on the essence of writing, on exactly *where* and *when* writing begins. Earlier in *Of Grammatology*, in fact, Derrida had emphasized the necessity of this kind of questioning:

> 'Where' and 'when' may open empirical questions: what, within history and within the world, are the places and the determined moments of the first phenomena of writing? These questions the investigation and research of facts must answer; history in the colloquial sense, what has hitherto been practised by nearly all archaeologists, epigraphists, and pre-historians who have interrogated the world's scripts.
>
> But the question of origin is at first confounded with the question of essence (. . .) One must know *what* writing *is* in order to ask – knowing what one is talking about and what *the question is* – where and when writing begins. What is writing? How can it be identified? What certitude of essence must guide the empirical investigation? (74–5; 110)

In the chapter on Lévi-Strauss, such questioning first arises in connection with another exemplary scene from *Tristes tropiques*, which involves the ethnologist playing with a group of Nambikwara children. Derrida quotes the passage describing the scene:

> One day, when I was playing with a group of children, a little girl was struck by one of her comrades. She ran to

me for protection and began to whisper something, a 'great secret', in my ear. As I did not understand I had to ask her to repeat it over and over again. Eventually her adversary found out what was going on, came up to me in a rage, and tried in her turn to tell me what seemed to be another secret. After a little while I was able to get to the bottom of the incident. The first little girl was trying to tell me her enemy's name, and when the enemy found out what was going on she decided to tell me the other girl's name, by way of reprisal. Thenceforward it was easy enough, though not very scrupulous, to egg the children on, one against the other, till in time I knew all of their names. When this was completed and we were all, in a sense, one another's accomplices, I soon got them to give me the adults' names too. When this [cabal] was discovered the children were reprimanded and my sources of information dried up. (111; 162–3)

Once again, in itself, this episode seems harmless enough: it shows the professional ethnologist at work even during his moments of play with the Nambikwara children – testing, observing, noting. However, the ethnologist's curiosity is also a violation in that he uncovers a system of secret naming which apparently it is forbidden to disclose: hence the reprimand the children receive from the adults. But Derrida is not content to remain at this empirical level of description, and questions Lévi-Strauss's construction and interpretation of the event. According to Lévi-Strauss, it is himself, as curious outsider, who is the agent of violence in his violation of the taboo of proper names: it is he who perturbs the Nambikwara social system from without. For Derrida, the ascription of violence and of guilt – the ethnologist assuming responsibility for the violation – is not so simple. *Within* the Nambikwara social system, he argues, the so-called 'proper names' have already been subjected to the violence of their obliteration, in their consignment to a secret system of classification:

The concept of the proper name, unproblematized as Lévi-Strauss uses it in *Tristes tropiques*, is therefore far from being simple and manageable. Consequently, the same may be said of the concepts of violence, ruse, perfidy, or oppression, that punctuate 'A Writing Lesson' a little further on. We have already noted that violence here does not unexpectedly break in all at once, starting from an original innocence whose nakedness is *surprised* at the very moment that the secret of the *so-called* proper names is violated. The structure of violence is complex and its possibility – writing – no less so.

There was in fact a first violence to be named. To name, to give names that it will on occasion be forbidden to pronounce, such is the originary violence of language which consists in inscribing within a difference, in classifying, in suspending the vocative absolute. To think the unique *within* the system, to inscribe it there, such is the gesture of the arche-writing: arche-violence, loss of the proper, of absolute proximity, of self-presence, in truth the loss of what has never taken place, of a self-presence which has never been given but only dreamed of and always already split, repeated, incapable of appearing to itself except in its own disappearance. Out of this arche-violence, forbidden and therefore confirmed by a second violence that is reparatory, protective, instituting the 'moral', prescribing the con-

32

cealment of writing and the effacement and obliteration of the so-called proper name which was already dividing the proper, a third violence can *possibly* emerge or not (an empirical possibility) within what is commonly called evil, war, indiscretion, rape; which consists of revealing by effraction the so-called proper name, the originary violence which has severed the proper from its property and its self-sameness. We could name a third violence of reflection, which denudes the native non-identity, classification as denaturation of the proper, and identity as the abstract moment of the concept. It is on this tertiary level, that of the empirical consciousness, that the common concept of violence (the system of the moral law and of transgression) whose possibility remains yet unthought, should no doubt be situated. The scene of proper names is written on this level; as will be later the writing lesson.

This last violence is all the more complex in its structure because it refers at the same time to the two inferior levels of arche-violence and of law. In effect, it reveals the first nomination which was already an expropriation, but it denudes also that which since then functioned as the proper, the so-called proper, substitute of the deferred proper, *perceived* by the *social* and *moral consciousness* as the proper, the reassuring seal of self-identity, the secret.

Empirical violence, war in the colloquial sense (ruse and perfidy of little girls, *apparent* ruse and perfidy of little girls, for the anthropologist will prove them innocent by showing himself as the true and only culprit; ruse and perfidy of the Indian chief playing at the comedy of writing, *apparent* ruse and perfidy of the Indian chief borrowing all his resources from the Occidental intrusion), which Lévi-Strauss always thinks of as an *accident*. An accident occurring, in his view, upon a terrain of innocence, in a 'state of culture' whose natural goodness had not yet been degraded. (111–12; 164–5)

Derrida therefore determines three levels of violence in the scene he names 'The Battle of Proper Names': the first and most primary, the most fundamental, is that of the institution of the proper name, which can only *be* a proper name as a function of its difference from other proper names. A proper name in itself means nothing, it can only perform its function of naming in relation to the other terms in a given system of classification: 'the proper name was never possible except through its functioning within a classification: and therefore within a system of differences' (109; 159). It is clear that what Derrida is presenting here is a *structural* definition of the proper name which, he reminds us, Lévi-Strauss himself subscribes to in other parts of his work. It will be remembered that Saussure's definition of language was that it is a system of differences, in which signification resides not in the terms themselves, but in the differential relations between them. Lévi-Strauss, it will again be remembered, adopted Saussure's model of the differential system and applied it to the kinship and classification systems of traditional societies. However, Saussure's, and, after him, Lévi-Strauss's conceptualization of difference in language is *phonocentric*, according to Derrida. As was learned above, Saussure's preliminary definition of the scope of the science of linguistics excludes and dismisses writing as a non-essential auxiliary to spoken language, as simply the external mediation of the authentic, living core of speech. Similarly, Lévi-Strauss's structuralism is a phoncentrism to the extent that its methods of analysis are modelled on those of phonology, the branch of linguistics that studies the sound systems of specific languages or of language in general. Derrida:

> In linguistics as well as in metaphysics, *phonologism* is undoubtedly the exclusion or abasement of writing. But it is also the granting of authority to a science which is held to be the model for all the so-called sciences of man. In both these senses Lévi-Strauss's structuralism is a phonologism. As for the 'models' of linguistics and phonology, what I have already brought up will not let me skirt around a structural anthropology upon which phonological science exercises so *declared* a fascination. (102; 151)

Derrida's conceptualization of difference, in contrast to that of Saussure and Lévi-Strauss, is predicated on a particular conception of writing. What exactly is the difference between these two ways of thinking difference? What is the specificity of 'writing', as Derrida understands it, that makes it a more appropriate means of describing the fundamental process at work in the Nambikwara system of nomination? One important aspect of Derrida's conception of writing is that it allows him to think precisely the category of violence that characterizes this fundamental process; it is impossible to think of a difference, of a system of differences, without the preliminary instance of their *inscription*, which involves an alteration of a hitherto undifferentiated 'space', in other words, a certain 'violence' done to it. This is clearly not 'violence' in the everyday, anthropological sense of the word, the visible and palpable violence of an aggression perpetrated by one person upon another, for example. Rather, it is the violence of a preliminary coding process without which systems of differentiation (in this instance the Nambikwara system of appellations) could not exist. Writing, in the common, everyday sense of word, dependent as it is on the inscription of a surface, the violent incision and separation of a medium (even the projection of characters upon a computer screen is not a *passive* process), functions therefore as a model of this more fundamentally violent inscription that Derrida above called 'arche-writing'. It is evident that speech – the voice – cannot serve as a model for such a process: according to the traditional (logo- and phonocentric) system of representation that opposes speech and writing, speech is transmitted through the transparent and impressionless medium of air, it leaves no trace; it is the ideal and immediate mediation of the soul, whereas writing inhabits the external, corporeal realm of matter. Simply put, then, it could be said that violence *is* (arche-) writing *is* difference.

The second level of violence Derrida delineates in his commentary of the 'Battle of the Proper Names' is that of the censorship, the covering over and effacement of the system of proper names instituted at the primary level just described. This is the instance of Nambikwara law, the interdiction of the utterance of the proper name, its violent consignment to secrecy. Again, in its invisibility, in its non-manifest operation, this is not violence in the common sense of the term: it is perhaps something akin to what sociologists would call 'structural' violence, inherent in the implicit social codes and classifications that regulate individual and collective behaviour and which are only made manifest through their violation. Such censorship is the precondition of the third and final level of violence, the manifest scene of violation, the ethnologist's indiscreet uncovering of what has been covered over. This is what Derrida terms *empirical* violence, which may or may not supervene upon the two, co-implicated levels – the institution of the system of proper names and the censorship of that institution – that precede it. This Derrida links with the violence of the 'Writing Lesson' that is to follow, the chief's subterfuge, his appropriation of writing and alleged expropriation of his people, which is a purely occasional and contingent, rather than a structural violence.

Derrida therefore locates an essential writing, an essential violence, at a level of determination more general and more abstract than that described in the scene of the 'Battle of Proper Names' or that of the 'Writing Lesson'. He accepts Lévi-Strauss's association of violence and writing, but with the qualification that there is violence and writing *before* the advent of language and writing in the common sense of the word: 'Anterior to the possibility of violence in the current and derivative sense, the sense used in "A Writing Lesson", there is, as the space of its possibility, the violence of the arche-writing, the violence of difference, of classification, and of the system of appellations' (110; 162).

Derrida's criticism of Lévi-Strauss is that not only does he fail to enquire into the essence of writing as violence, he also chooses to ignore even the *empirical* manifestations of violence in Nambikwara society:

If the 'Lesson' is to be believed, the Nambikwara did not

know violence before writing; nor hierarchization, since that is quickly assimilated into exploitation. Round about the 'Lesson', it suffices to open *Tristes tropiques* and the thesis at any page to find striking evidence to the contrary. We are dealing here not only with a strongly hierarchized society, but with a society where relationships are marked with a spectacular violence. As spectacular as the innocent and tender frolics evoked at the beginning of the 'Lesson', and that we were thus justified in considering as the calculated premises of a loaded argument. (135; 196)

Derrida draws attention to an episode related in *Tristes tropiques*, but which is not part of the actual 'demonstration' of the 'Writing Lesson': there are in fact descriptions of violent feuds between members of the community, as a result of which at one point, for example, the ethnologist is approached by a number of individuals who ask him to poison another member of the tribe. Lévi-Strauss's Rousseauist myth of an innocent society corrupted from without is thus at variance with his own depiction of that society. As Derrida shows, Lévi-Strauss *declares* that the Nambikwara are good, but what he actually *describes* is a society marked – like all societies – by violence, both structural (an extremely hierarchized social structure) and interpersonal.

It would be useful to dwell an instant on what I have just described as Lévi-Strauss's 'Rousseauist myth', as the link Derrida establishes between the two thinkers is an important element not only in his situating of Lévi-Strauss within a certain tradition of philosophical thought, but also for the further understanding of his general theory of writing. As

Derrida reminds us, Lévi-Strauss presents his own anthropological project as directly inspired by the work and thought of Jean-Jacques Rousseau, whom he designates as the founder and spiritual father of modern anthropology. In his famous essay on the origins of human inequality, the *Second Discourse*, Rousseau had argued that the state perhaps best suited to individual freedom and authentic human relations was one intermediate between the state of nature and the social (civilized) state. In the lengthy meditation on the vocation and meaning of modern anthropology that occupies the closing chapters of *Tristes tropiques*, Lévi-Strauss agrees with Rousseau's diagnosis, and suggests that the hypothetical social state described in the *Second Discourse* would probably be approximate to the level of cultural development we today associate with the Neolithic period. At the most manifest level, therefore, that of a certain ideology of the primitivist utopia, there is a strong affinity between Lévi-Strauss and Rousseau, their filiation is a clear and explicit one. In this connection, Derrida speaks of Lévi-Strauss's 'declared and militant Rousseauism' (106; 155).

Apart from this spiritual or ideological affinity, however, there is also a more abstract, one could say, *structural* similarity between Lévi-Strauss and Rousseau, in terms of their conceptualization of how the ideal state or system is disturbed, how one passes from the innocent and the authentic, the pure and the immediate, to the corrupt, the mediated and the alienated. For both Lévi-Strauss and Rousseau, Derrida argues, such a transition is never a natural consequence of the system itself; rather, it is always precipitated by some external perturbation, some external aggression to the system. This is the case with Lévi-Strauss's

'Writing Lesson', as we have seen. His tendentious representation of the 'innocence' of the Nambikwara is the indispensable basis of his distinction between an internal and an external space, 'good' and 'evil', the internal paradise of Nambikwara society and the external aggression of writing, the poisoned gift of civilization. Without writing, Nambikwara society remains in a kind of prehistorical state of limbo, an eternal present, blessed in its poverty and its ignorance. With the advent of writing, it enters history, which brings inequality and exploitation. Luckily, according to Lévi-Strauss, the Nambikwara intuitively sense the danger of this and abandon the chief, thereby gaining temporary respite from the encroachments of civilization.

Derrida's corrective to Lévi-Strauss's dichotomy of internal and external space (innocence-corruption, proximity-alienation, authenticity-artifice, etc.) is to suggest that it is basically a *projection* outside of the system described (Nambikwara society) of something which is already at work in the system, is part of the system, inherent to the dynamic of the system. This kind of projection is not peculiar to Lévi-Strauss, but is a habitual reflex of logocentric framing: that which in effect is native to a system, essential to its very existence and persistence (here, 'writing' and 'violence') is considered an inessential and even dangerous *supplement* to it. A binary opposition is therefore established between a pure, inner core or origin (in language, voice), and the externalized mediation of this core or origin (writing). But as Derrida shows in the different cases of Lévi-Strauss, Rousseau, and Saussure, the very possibility of supplementation exposes an essential lack at the heart of the supposedly autonomous and self-sufficient system.

Writing, difference, violence, are not something that *happens* to a previously pure and intact system, they are not something that supervenes from without. To use Derrida's own formulation, writing, difference, violence are *always already* there, at the origin, from the origin, which means in effect that there is no (pure) origin.

It can be seen here that Derrida's problematization of the notion of origin adds a *temporal* dimension to the structure of 'writing', as it is gradually emerging from this commentary. Let us recapitulate. To the question *where* does writing begin, we saw that Derrida responded by extending both the empirical and the structural field of writing: writing in the common sense of the term occupied a terrain wider than that of conventional scriptural systems; writing in the general sense of the term operated at a level of determination deeper than that of empirical writing, indeed was the very condition of possibility of empirical writing and of language in general. Now, in the present instance, to the question *when* does writing begin, Derrida's response is: always already. To posit an origin of writing is meaningless when one is dealing with a continuum of writing. Writing is a structure of *all* complex systems at *all* of their levels.

The temporal dimension Derrida gives to his model of writing reminds us that this 'writing' which violently differentiates (writing = violence = difference), which generates the differences that are constitutive of complex systems is not, by analogy with writing in the common sense of the term, a tangible or visible residue, it is not a static 'script'. Rather, it is a process, a movement, which institutes difference while at the same time holding it in reserve, deferring its presentation or operation. Derrida uses the term *différance* to describe this process, which he frequently refers to as the *movement* of differance. This neologism is derived from the French verb 'différer', which means to defer, to adjourn, to put off. Derrida's substantivization of the verb could be translated as something like 'deferment' in English, but this loses a whole complex of associations peculiar to the original French. The suffix '-ance', which in French is more precisely a substantivization of the present continuous tense ('différant', deferring), connotes a sense of temporal extension impossible to render in English. Moreover, in French the term is phonetically indistinguishable from the word 'différence'. It is therefore through the essentially untranslatable linguistic device of homophony that Derrida establishes a conceptual link between the notion of writing as (spatial) difference and writing as (temporal) deferment: writing *is* difference *is* deferment (differance).

A similar kind of linguistic overdetermination applies in the case of another term which is central to Derrida's theory or model of writing: 'trace'. In a sense, the concept of the trace could be considered to be more essential still to Derrida's model than the concept of 'writing', to the extent that there can be no writing without trace, without violent inscription, without residue. But again, Derrida's understanding of trace is a dynamic one, that is to say, the trace is as much movement as it is substance, as much *protention* towards a future as it is *retention* of a past. Derrida repeatedly insists that the trace is *nothing*, it is not, properly speaking, an entity or a substance. Again, he uses an interesting linguistic configuration to express this dual structure, associating the French word 'trace' with its reverse anagram, 'écart' (distance, difference, divergence, interval, space, spacing). If one accepts the logic of this linguistically arbitrary association ('trace'-'écart'), it is a useful way of conceptualizing the essentially double-bound structure of writing: the trace is simultaneously and inseparably inscription and interval, residue and difference. To repeat Derrida's own formulation, cited above, it could be said that the trace is *always already* differing from itself, there is no original (substantial) trace. The following passage, quoted from an earlier chapter of the *Grammatology* on the concept of difference in linguistics, usefully summarizes Derrida's thinking concerning the trace:

Here the appearing and functioning of difference presupposes an originary synthesis not preceded by any absolute simplicity. Such would be the originary trace. Without a retention in the minimal unit of temporal experience, without a trace retaining the other as other in the same, no difference would do its work and no meaning would appear. It is not the question of a constituted difference here, but rather, before all determination of the content, of the *pure* movement which produces difference. *The (pure) trace is differance.* It does not depend on any sensible plenitude, audible or visible, phonic or graphic. It is, on the contrary, the condition of such a plenitude. Although it *does not exist*, although it is never a *being-present* outside of all plenitude, its possibility is by rights anterior to all that one calls sign (signified/signifier, content/expression, etc.), concept or operation, motor or sensory. This differance is therefore not more sensible than intelligible and it permits the articulation of signs among themselves within the same abstract order – a phonic or graphic text for example – or between two orders of expression. It permits the articulation of speech and writing – in the colloquial sense – as it founds the metaphysical opposition between the sensible and the intelligible, then between signifier and signified, expression and content, etc. If language were not already, in that sense, a writing, no derived 'notation' would be possible; and the classical problem of relationships between speech and writing could not arise. (62–3; 91–2)

The preceding exposition might seem extremely abstract and far removed from the human situation we began with, Lévi-Strauss's parable of the 'Writing Lesson'. It represents a recession, a pushing back of the scene of writing from the common, everyday understanding of the word to the very conditions of possibility of 'writing' in general. However, it should not be thought that Derrida's questioning concerning writing is restricted to a purely metaphysical problem, of interest only to philosophers. In fact, from the very start of the *Grammatology*, Derrida situates his enquiry in a context wider than that of the academic discipline of philosophy itself. His own focus on writing, he insists, is not an isolated gesture, but reflects and is part of a more general revolution in modern thought. There is first the localized shift, within the structuralist paradigm, from 'language' to 'writing'. As was explained above, the structuralism of Lévi-Strauss and others was based on the application of a model of difference derived from structural linguistics. For the structuralists, the term 'language' applied not only to verbal communication, but to any complex or system: everything was, or was structured like, a language. However, in the introduction to *Of Grammatology*, Derrida notes a subtle shift of emphasis with respect to the linguistic analogy, as it is used in structuralism: 'For some time now, as a matter of fact, here and there, by a gesture and for motives that are profoundly necessary (...) one says "language" for action, movement, thought, reflection, consciousness, unconsciousness, experience, affectivity, etc. Now we tend to say "writing" for all that and more' (9; 19). The shift of emphasis is not simply a reflection of developments internal to philosophy and the human sciences. Derrida thinks that the use of the linguistic, or now more precisely, the scriptural model is central to the major advances in postwar science, above all in new disciplines such as molecular biology, information theory and cybernetics. He continues: 'The contemporary biologist speaks of writing and *pro-gram* in relation to the most elementary processes of information within the living cell. And finally, whether it has essential limits or not, the entire field covered by the cybernetic *program* would be the field of writing' (ibid.).

It is important to remember how recent these advances were at the time Derrida was writing *Of Grammatology*. To take the example of molecular biology, Watson and Crick's work on the structure of DNA was barely ten years old, while the work of the French biologists Jacob and Monod on RNA 'messenger' was still more recent. The conceptualization of the genetic code as a form of 'script', involving the combination, transposition, punctuation and deletion of 'characters', was obviously of capital interest to philosophers interested in language, and seemed to offer further confirmation of the linguistic turn already initiated by structuralism. Derrida's model of writing as a dynamic process of differance-difference is in fact very close to the idea of DNA as both a conservative *and* a metamorphic code, or, in cybernetics, the notion of the cybernetic circuit as having a memory based on the *movement* of information around the circuit, rather than on the static storage of information.

It is important also to remember the specificity of the sciences in question. Biology and cybernetics occupy what might be termed the 'soft' end of the so-called 'hard' sciences, and are of interest to philosophy and the human sciences precisely because they touch more immediately upon questions concerning the 'human' and the 'natural'. In cybernetics, for example, the preoccupation with information transfer and auto-mobile processes (communication and control) in animals, machines and humans offers new ways of thinking the relationships between the animal and the human, the human and the technological. The latter question in particular, the question concerning technology, reminds us that Derrida's own thinking on writing was not only inspired by scientific theory but also, inseparably, by the *practice* of the new information and communication technologies developed in the postwar period. In a very real sense, it is the presence and pervasiveness of this new ambient technology which makes possible the grammatological enquiry into the essence of writing. One can only properly think beyond logocentric categories such as the opposition of speech and writing in a context where such oppositions have been *defamiliarized*, stripped of their aura of self-evidence through their confrontation with a generalized technology of 'writing'.

Derrida's diagnosis of a certain 'end' of logocentric metaphysics is therefore, inseparably, part of this more general transformation of modern technological culture.

If the postwar development of the informal sciences is a cardinal reference point for Derrida's theory of writing, it is nevertheless an influence and a context which is evoked rather than treated in detail in the pages of the *Grammatology*. A more important and substantial point of reference in this respect is the work of the French ethnologist and prehistorian André Leroi-Gourhan (1911–86). In his book *Gesture and Speech* (1964–5), Leroi-Gourhan demonstrated how, from the long-term perspective of human evolution, manual technology had played a crucial role in the development of human intelligence and the capacity for symbolic representation. According to Leroi-Gourhan, such development was only possible through the close and mutually reinforcing interaction of hand and brain over the millennia. This natural historical account of the evolution of symbolic systems is consistent with Derrida's understanding of 'writing' as a *continuum*, extending from the 'biological' to the 'human' to the 'technological'. As he notes, Leroi-Gourhan does not simply extend the capacity for writing to the whole of humankind (as we saw Derrida himself doing in the case of Lévi-Strauss), but also refers to a more general process of 'graphical' archivation essential to the articulation of life itself:

> But it is not enough to denounce ethnocentrism and to define anthropological unity by the disposition of writing. Leroi-Gourhan no longer describes the unity of man and the human adventure thus by the simple possibility of the *graphie* in general; rather as a stage or an

47

articulation in the history of life – of what I have called difference – as the history of the *grammè*. Instead of having recourse to the concepts that habitually serve to distinguish man from other living beings (instinct and intelligence, absence or presence of speech, of society, of economy, etc. etc.), the notion of *program* is invoked. It must of course be understood in the cybernetic sense, but cybernetics is itself intelligible only in terms of a history of the possibilities of the trace as the unity of a double movement of protention and retention. This movement goes far beyond the possibilities of the 'intentional consciousness'. It is an emergence that makes the *grammè* appear *as such* (that is to say according to a new structure of nonpresence) and undoubtedly makes possible the emergence of the systems of writing in the narrow sense. Since 'genetic inscription' and the 'short programmatic chains' regulating the behaviour of the amoeba or the annelid up to the passage beyond alphabetic writing to the orders of the logos and of a certain *homo sapiens*, the possibility of the *grammè* structures the movement of its history according to rigorously original levels, types, and rhythms. But one cannot think them without the most general concept of the *grammè*. That is irreducible and impregnable. If the expression ventured by Leroi-Gourhan is accepted, one could speak of a 'liberation of memory', of an exteriorization always already begun but always larger than the trace which, beginning from the elementary programs of so-called 'instinctive' behaviour up to the constitution of electronic card-indexes and reading machines, enlarges differance and the possibility of putting in reserve: it at once and in the same movement constitutes and effaces so-called conscious subjectivity, its logos, and its theological attributes. (84; 125–6)

This extremely condensed passage brings together a number of points concerning Derrida's theory of writing, which might be summarized as follows:

1. Writing in the general sense of the term extends beyond even the widest definition of empirical systems of writing; rather it is the condition of possibility of writing in the common sense of the term, and indeed of language in general.

2. Writing in the general sense of the term has a dual structure, or more precisely, to use Derrida's expression, movement: it is both residual and dynamic, retentive and protentive. The trace or the *grammè*, as Derrida calls it (Greek: *gramma*, letter, writing, a small weight, hence 'grammatology'), is not a substance present here and now (one cannot *see*, *feel* or *hear* difference): it is differance, that is, spatial difference and temporal difference (deferment). This structure, or rather, structuring principle is common to all complex systems involving the recording, storage and communication of information.

3. The movement of writing in the general sense of the term (trace, *grammè*, differance) is not something that proceeds from 'life' as we know it. Given what we now know about the structure of the genetic code, it would be tempting here to posit the biological as a kind of first and final instance: the various forms of 'writing' or 'memory' that structure and extend the human from this vital base could be seen as a continuation and modulation of the

basic 'writing' or 'text' of DNA. This is not, however, Derrida's argument. As he notes, one cannot conceptualize the different stages of the evolution of human life without a general concept of the trace or *grammè*, without the concept of differance, which precedes the instance of 'life' and makes it possible.

4. While Derrida's conception of writing is in one sense transcendental, that is, it places the instance of writing beyond or behind the scene of our everyday experience of phenomena, it is not a philosophical abstraction or speculation, even less a quasi-theological reference to an ineffable, extra-temporal essence. The 'nonpresence' of the *grammè*, as Derrida describes it here, in contrast with classical philosophical transcendentalism, is situated *in* history, that of the evolution of the trace, an evolution which precedes even the process of so-called 'natural' history. So Derrida's theory of writing is at once a *structural* one (describing the essence of writing as (violent) inscription, difference and deferment) and a *historical* one (describing the continuum of the trace from the pre-biological to the bio-anthropological to the diverse articulations and extensions of the bio-anthropological).

5. From this structural and historical perspective, the question of *where* and *when* writing begins, posed earlier, becomes superfluous, or at best, relative. Derrida's conception of writing defamiliarizes the customary distinctions made between speech and writing, life and death, presence and absence, the human and the animal, the human and the technological, and emphasizes instead their necessary co-implication and continuity. The various (logocentric)

philosophies of presence which prioritize the living, human, individual (intentional) consciousness and treat as simply secondary and derived any of its external mediations, precisely require such distinctions and demarcations in order to maintain their fiction of the pure and integrally self-conscious subject that is commonly called 'man'.

This last point concerning Derrida's critique of logocentrism brings us back, finally, to the more general question of the philosophical programme pursued in *Of Grammatology*, and the mode of critical analysis Derrida calls 'deconstruction'. Since its inception in the 1960s, the word itself has been so widely used – and, it must be said, misused – in certain forms of critical theoretical discourse that the force and complexity of Derrida's original formulation has frequently been all but lost. It would be useful, therefore, to attempt to bring together the different elements of Derrida's approach, as it has emerged from the preceding analysis of his theory of writing, in order to determine exactly what deconstruction is and what it does.

First, it is clear that deconstruction is not, as is sometimes assumed, a purely adversarial form of philosophical critique. Its priority is not the destruction or demolition of a given philosophical opponent. Derrida's critique of Lévi-Strauss in *Of Grammatology* is, by all accounts, a devastating one, but its first and final intention is not to singularize the individual 'Lévi-Strauss' as an instance of inconsistency and error. On the contrary, as we have seen, Derrida's gesture is to treat Lévi-Strauss – like Saussure, like Rousseau – as an example or symptom of a way of thinking more pervasive and more persistent than any one individual thinker, a kind of metaphysical field of force that would enclose and shape – constrain – our apprehension and conceptualization of the world. Derrida explains this approach in the preamble to his reading of Lévi-Strauss and Rousseau:

> The names of authors or of doctrines have here no substantial value. They indicate neither identities nor causes (…) The indicative value that I attribute to them is first the name of a problem. If I provisionally authorize myself to treat this historical structure by fixing my attention on philosophical or literary texts, it is not for the sake of identifying in them the origin, cause, or equilibrium of the structure. But as I also do not think that these texts are the simple *effects* of structure, in any sense of the word; as I think that *all concepts hitherto proposed in order to think the articulation of a discourse and of an historical totality are caught within the metaphysical closure that I question here*, as we do not know of any other concepts and cannot produce any others, and indeed shall not produce so long as this closure limits our discourse: as the primordial and indispensable phase, in fact and in principle, of the development of this problematic, consists in questioning the internal structure of these texts as symptoms; as that is the only condition for determining these symptoms *themselves* in the totality of their metaphysical appurtenance; I draw my argument from them in order to isolate Rousseau, and, in Rousseauism, the theory of writing. (99; 147–8)

Hence Derrida does not transitively 'deconstruct' Lévi-Strauss or Rousseau or Saussure; rather, he uncovers the conceptual and argumentative reflexes, the sequences and associations of ideas which precede and condition the thinking of these authors, and which operate as a kind of unconscious that speaks *through* them and almost in spite of them. As he notes above, this process of disclosure consists in questioning the 'internal structure' of the texts chosen as symptoms of the cognitive field he calls 'logocentrism'. We have seen a working example of this in Derrida's reading of Lévi-Strauss. His patient negotiation of Lévi-Strauss's theory of writing lets Lévi-Strauss himself speak – frequently and at length – in the form of direct quotation and detailed paraphrase, so that Lévi-Strauss's text could in a sense be said to 'deconstruct' itself, the critique of his theory of writing arising from the immanent contradictions of that text. Rather than direct refutation, therefore, deconstruction could be described as a form of critical dialogue, which uses the examples of particular case histories (here Lévi-Strauss) as symptoms of a more general configuration or structure.

A second important point concerning deconstruction is that it is not merely a critique or contestation of the tradition of thought Derrida names 'logocentrism'. Derrida questions the traditional oppositions of speech and writing (presence and absence, essential and contingent, primary and auxiliary, etc.), not in order simply to reverse or overturn these oppositions, but rather in order to *displace* them. As we have seen, his critique of Lévi-Strauss's symptomatic rejection of writing is inseparable from his questioning of what writing actually *is*. The second stage or moment of deconstruction would therefore be the widening of the frames of reference, the loosening of the rigid systems of oppositions, which habitually shape and constrain our understanding of the world. This leads to a more general theory of writing as the fundamental structure of complex systems, as an essential continuum rather than a discrete and isolable practice or phenomenon. It is important to emphasize the extent to which deconstruction is embedded in the question of writing as it is explored in *Of Grammatology* and other, related texts of the same period, since there is often a tendency to decontextualize deconstruction, to present it as a method of critical analysis separate from the theory of writing which is its original and essential corollary.

A third and final point concerning deconstruction is the importance of *language*. We have already seen how Derrida's reading of Lévi-Strauss is attentive to the rhetorical as well the conceptual dimension of his theory of writing, indeed how these two aspects – the so-called 'literary' and the 'philosophical' – are shown to be inseparable. For Derrida, language is never the transparent and neutral mediator of thought; the concept is always subject to refraction in its passage through this opaque and overdetermined medium of communication. Derrida's sensitivity to the linguistic and the literary in the texts of the thinkers he deals with could be said to apply, reflexively, to his own writing. His formulation of the theory of writing, for example, does not conform to the canons of what might be characterized as traditional philosophical discourse. In fact, nowhere is there a systematic *definition* of writing in the general sense of the word. Derrida does not construct his theory of writing axiomatically, from the bottom up, as it were, but rather from the top down: first through the process of dialogue noted above, dismantling and displacing the conceptual infrastructures of traditional metaphysics; second, through a linguistic negotiation of 'writing' that involves the *pluralization* of its attributes rather than their fixation and substantivization. Thus one obtains a complex of associated terms that constitute not so much a description of 'writing' as an approximation of its problematic essence: inscription-violence-trace(-'écart')-arche-writing-*grammè*-difference(-differance). This strategy of linguistic dispersal could be said to be a central feature of deconstruction, which attempts to circumvent, if not transcend, the essentializing discourse of traditional metaphysics.

To conclude, it is necessary once more to widen the focus of our discussion to consider the more general context of Derrida's critique of Lévi-Strauss in *Of Grammatology*. On the one hand, the theory of writing that emerges from this critique is universal, to the extent that it describes an essential structure or principle independent of any specification of historical context. On the other hand, the critique itself – like any philosophical discourse – is necessarily situated in a particular context, with all the complications such a situation entails. As was noted earlier, in 1960s France the context was the hegemony of structuralism and the human sciences, as incarnated in the figure of Lévi-Strauss and the discipline of ethnology. Placed in this context, Derrida's critical engagement with Lévi-Strauss in *Of Grammatology* could therefore be seen as the decisive response of philosophy to the challenge of structuralism and the human sciences. Whereas Sartre's criticism of structuralism – its neglect of concrete relations and its reduction of human agency and historical process – remained squarely within a certain humanistic tradition of philosophy, it could be said that Derrida engages structuralism on its own ground, at the level of its discourse and its concepts. His deconstruction of Lévi-Strauss's theory of writing reveals a surprising lack of rigour in a discourse which was asserting the scientific credentials of its own concepts whilst claiming to have left behind the categories and abstractions of traditional philosophical discourse. His extension of the field of writing – both empirical and essential – exposes the basic ethnocentrism of Lévi-Strauss's distinction between literate and nonliterate cultures. In doing this, he strikes at the heart of the human scientific enterprise as represented in ethnology, whose very object of enquiry (the nonliterate culture) was based on this distinction and whose moral and humanistic mission consisted precisely in its critique of ethnocentrism. The importance of the historical conjuncture of the question of ethnocentrism, the notion of ethnology as human science and the idea of a certain 'end' of traditional metaphysics – all of these framed by the still recent experience of postwar decolonization – is underlined by Derrida in a text on Lévi-Strauss and structuralism written at the same time as the critique in *Of Grammatology*:

> One of [the human sciences] perhaps occupies a privileged place – ethnology. In fact one can assume that ethnology could have been born as a science only at the moment when a decentering had come about: at the moment when European culture – and, in consequence, the history of metaphysics and of its concepts – had been *dislocated*, driven from its locus, and forced to stop considering itself as the culture of reference. This moment is not first and foremost a moment of philosophical or scientific discourse. It is also a moment which is political, economic, technical, and so forth. One can say with total security that there is nothing fortuitous

about the fact that the critique of ethnocentrism – the very condition for ethnology – should be systematically and historically contemporaneous with the destruction of the history of metaphysics. Both belong to one and the same era. Now, ethnology – like any science – comes about within the element of discourse. And it is primarily a European science employing traditional concepts, however much it may struggle against them. Consequently, whether he wants to or not – and this does not depend on a decision on his part – the ethnologist accepts into his discourse the premises of ethnocentrism at the very moment when he denounces them. This necessity is irreducible; it is not a historical contingency. We ought to consider all its implications very carefully. But if no one can escape this necessity, and if no one is therefore responsible for giving in to it, however little he may do so, this does not mean that all the ways of giving in to it are of equal pertinence. The quality and fecundity of a discourse are perhaps measured by the critical rigour with which this relation to the history of metaphysics and to inherited concepts is thought. Here it is a question both of a critical relation to the language of the social sciences and a critical responsibility of the discourse itself. It is a question of explicitly and systematically posing the problem of the status of a discourse which borrows from a heritage the resources necessary for the deconstruction of that heritage itself. A problem of *economy* and *strategy*.[2]

As Derrida's reading of Lévi-Strauss in *Of Grammatology* demonstrates, the 'critical responsibility' which should be the preliminary concern of all human scientific discourse is signally absent from Lévi-Strauss's theory of writing and the various narrative and argumentative configurations that serve it. Indeed, in the introductory remarks to his reading of Lévi-Strauss and Rousseau, Derrida notes that: 'In Western and notably French thought, the dominant discourse – let us call it "structuralism" – remains caught, by an entire layer, sometimes the most fecund, of its stratification, within the metaphysics – logocentrism – which at the same time one claims rather precipitately to have "gone beyond"' (99; 148). We have seen how Derrida himself turns Lévi-Strauss's parable of the 'Writing Lesson', Lévi-Strauss's lesson on writing, into a lesson in thinking, thinking critically about the essence of writing and thinking critically about the demarcations and categorizations that normally structure our perception and comprehension of the world. The lesson given by philosophy to the human sciences, as exemplified in Derrida's reading of Lévi-Strauss, is that one cannot simply step outside of a philosophical tradition and reason independently of it. It teaches us that there will always be a need for the critical reflex which is essential to philosophy, that a science that does not think – even if prefaced with the epithet 'human' – should not have the last word.

NOTES

1. *De la grammatologie* (Paris, Minuit, 1967); translated by Gayatri Chakravorty Spivak (Baltimore, The Johns Hopkins University Press, 1976). Page references for *Of Grammatology* are given in the main text, in each case the reference for the original French text following that of the English translation.

2. *Writing and Difference*, translated by Alan Bass (London, Routledge, 1978), p. 282; *L'écriture et la différence* (Paris, Seuil, 1967), p. 414.